Flight Patt

(Prestatyn '91)

For Kate Thomas here and Rich Baker over there.

Flight Patterns

JOHN DAVIES

John Davies

SEREN BOOKS

Seren Books is the book imprint of
Poetry Wales Press Ltd
Andmar House, Tondu Road
Bridgend, Mid-Glamorgan

British Library Cataloguing in Publication Data
for this title is available from the British Library
Data Office.

ISBN 1-85411-044-6

The publisher acknowledges the financial support of the
Welsh Arts Council

Typeset in 10 1/2 Point Palatino by Megaron, Cardiff

Printed by John Penry Press, Swansea

CONTENTS

1.

11.

1

Champagne

Night opened when the pub
shut, so cold I couldn't
face the moon revolving
the town like a piece of glass
for its neon flash.
The place, capsized,
leaned on chimneys.
Behind leafy curtains, houses
flushed with old red tile
kept an eye on their gravelled
drives. No walkers.

Dr. Price would have yelled
his *Song of the Primitive
Bard to the Moon*.
In that fox-skin cap, paws
scampering, he'd have preached
from his goat cart, rattled
streets with notions.
I stumbled, silent, on.
Near death, he drank champagne,
breath isn't everything.
He let the future know,
those keen on different shades
of grey, there's another way,
that each man has his Price.

It wasn't listening.
Towed behind tv. cameras,
homes navigated rivers of tea.
Trees spun shadow wheels,
a car half-buried chewed
its own grille, then our door caved
in and the cat on the piano
played the dark.

Pursuit

I've been reading letters my father sent
after D-Day, the edging inland
through Normandy under fire from mosquitoes
then rain, sleep chopped in fragments
("All the guns in France won't wake me")
and, after stand-to, breakfast canned.

"We have come back from the front." Censored,
stray shellfire bursts through anyhow.
A lot's buried. He bathed "in our English Channel",
sang *Lledrod* in an apple orchard.
I'd ask if Collinge made it, Smith,
but all those guns wouldn't wake him now —

and at least one risk made him blunt:
the abbey at Mont St. Michel "is treacherous
without a guide. There are secret passages
so one can easily get lost." *About the front...*
I'd have probed, though we are too slow
to ask the past much, slipping from us.

Still turning the dark side from his family,
he stored the letters in this book he'd keep
safe. He knew us, I think. We knew
the half of him. What he let us see
was the orchard, light cover, you'd have
to guess the dugout seven feet deep,

and I know now that when we let
silence speak it didn't, would not
speak for us, marching to the old tune
Sons and Fathers that we couldn't forget.
So looking at my daughter
suddenly I need to say something but what.

Flights
(for Rich)

Off Route 101 near Spanaway, your father's duck farm
blights an intersection — can't miss it, you said.
Correct. When I slam the car shut, ducks squall back.
Your Dodge isn't here. No one answers the bell.
Out in the rippling field pegged down by sheds,
footsteps have been and gone, it's an ancient
railroad accident, bent roofs, windows cobweb-crazed
over buckets brimming with grass. I peer in,
expect some unhinged Birdman flopped
where only feathers stir. On a table squats his cap.
Overalls look lived in. Chisels curl dry lips.
Dim rows of eggs the local Vietnamese love raw
curve a path back to the house and
you turn up at last, sensation in the duck world.
"You've not missed much. Dad's a mean old guy.
Likes the British though — was over there once."
My road back speeds him out of mind.

*

Three years on and you're coming over,
December. By now I'm unsure who'll arrive
though your letters sound like you, shaking
my breakfast trance back down that year of freeways.

Nostalgic, for once your father's opened up:
you'll find no crime here, land unspoiled.
An eden. His war in England was his happy time
not just for the Thunderbolts he sharpened,
young bloods blown free to a warrior airbase.
Later when airmail letters landed in Spanaway
one by one, mid-table your mother parked them.
But he'd not react. His brother told you this.
Only the fire opened them.

You've dragged that damaged thigh up hillsides,
braved black pudding. Careful on stony ground,
we've done the castles. By now we need more space
or less. When you turned up that address
your father explained in code ("Check it out
if you're... Name's Kath") as he glanced elsewhere,
I gladly fetched the map. Dawley's two hours
south-east and it's movement handles distance
so that's how, after misdirections, dead-ends,
this day of frost gone marble blue,
in undergrowth that reclaimed an airbase,
unbarbing wire and sacking the ordnance store,
we send up pigeons to reconnoitre cloud.
In a tunnel your flash-bulb fires rust.
And yellow sweat, look, of varnish still.
Over grassy tarmac around stumps,
our paths converge not only on your father
again where he'd find too little himself.
We fill up winter space, criss-crossing.

Later: "That Kath," you grunt. "She'll be shining
young, still hot for nylons." As we enter Dawley.

*

A good flight back to Washington, you write
of a distance shorter measured in air.
"Gone absolutely British. Bought a special hat
for the feather." Coming from bed dressed
in himself, your father asked so you told him,
expecting him to have known. Yes, went to Dawley.
No, she wasn't there. Silence sent surprise both ways.
"Never seen that sadness in him before."

What he'd expected after all those years
wasn't all those years.
Clipped wings in a cluttered field at evening
flare, then settle as trees bank in on the house.

"Anyway, keep writing." Which I will,
for now wondering how that pigeon feather — I took
one too from the base — looks on your special hat.

Airmail

Our Singles leader
who came to us via hinduism
left in August for L.A. —
another lesson

in letting go —
so we formed a group to visit
but he's wrapped up in his job.
He said to phone.

I miss mother still.
I was asleep when she died,
she was dead when I woke up.
That picnic

when I went to shoot
the rapids while you and she talked?
Where the rapids began I stopped
in my rubber tube,

could not go back
and wouldn't let go till you
jumped in. God's with me through all
my ditsy times.

Just three of us
showed up at the movies this week
out of a lot who said they would.
If better offers come,

they go with the best
deal. We had a lecture at Singles
about the Peter Pan syndrome and
I think accepting

the child in us
is great but American singles need
to accept responsibility. I'm
here most nights.

Friends gave me a date
for my birthday, he wasn't what
I'd choose. Doesn't read and cannot
spell these words: ambivalent,

effrontery, celibate.
He still hasn't finished the children's
book I gave him. Nearly everyone
is astonished

at the growth
I've undergone. My dinosaur book display
is creating sales at the store. If you see
the others, say

hi for me, say
everything's fine. Which it is
for now, though I'm not
the Jayne they knew,

Howard

In town, a long sad face shunting a rumble
turned into Howard Roberts from Philadelphia
tracking his roots. I owe America.
Tour buses roared, sawing Wales in half
as we talked, and, keen, I showed him our pet castle.
Ghost yawns closing one eye then his other
suggested that belonging might come pricey.

West in thrashed acres where he found
most valleys are depressions between faults,
farms and quarries mourned by sheds
proved rain's not always kind to withered roots.

The bar foamed. Stan folded in laughter, an ancient
head juggling false teeth, a Punch and Judy show.
Howard wasn't unimpressed but shunned groups of more
than one — eyes sad about their wicked weight
of brow turned down his mouth, the grin a wince.
His voice trailing off in search of entrances
or exits said it wasn't a past he needed.

He stayed long enough anyway to lose his tan,
sing with the choir once and leave antique shops
looted. Whole bunches of choice bric
and brac were bedded lovingly for transplant
so though he found not a single root
quite a lot of the old country went with him, you bet.

Arrival

Flung down the mountain slide, light
  jabbed roads
    quivering, burst cars. Doors opened
  on blast. The town sleek as a full wallet
    spread for strangers, shine
outdazzled, flared.

All spring, sun must have sharpened glass.
  A rising
      against walls, against white skin,
    when it came smoke was on its breath:
      watch difference burn you up.
Midday curfew began.

Shadows flattened were dragged away
  by trees.
    Late afternoon, past crouched houses
  with porches pulled low over their eyes,
    clouds staggered from cover,
light flashed in pursuit.

That August I watched mostly from the bottom
  of a swimming pool.
    Over and over, legs smashed through
  the lid. Glassblown bodies tumbled
    where I was tile and pale blue water,
too pale, out of touch.

Fires

Yesterday, mist hazed the mountains
but no, Rob said, it was California burning.
I wouldn't have known. Hoarse forest-eaters
were breathing blackmail on three States.

Today though, a river following our road like a dolphin
dived past poles shouldering telegraph wire
and small towns flagged us down, streets broad as open hands.
The parks had pioneer relics, a grindstone, hoisted bell.
On a grass square, ranked seats at Payson
wore the flag's colours, paths slipped a world in edgewise.
Trees spurted sun. Between *For Sale* signs
old as prayers and the highway murmuring Go, what survived
seemed so entire of itself, it could last forever.

Haze lasted too, from the edge of things
kept coming in. Burned air overloaded
had dropped again long distance.
At dusk, with the first crackle of autumn
rubbing green edges red,
bushes along the road were ghosts.

Static

Midwinter, when snow built a cave
                lit by the screen
we warmed our eyes on, tanned
                      heads crowded in
and evangelists, gold-fingered,
                          prayed we'd been born
again yesterday. Static's
                dwarf lightning
shook hands. Positives switched
                to negatives.
In boxed space were jabs
                to retreat from
(aliveness of rubbed crackling!)
                not just yet. Voices
next door: the wall's version
                of people. Overhead,
mountains caught light each day
                and threw shadows.
They smoked clouds only, drank in
                just the view — you get
tired of them, mountains, flexing
                their good examples.
Man's niche should direct his grasp
                or what's a valley for?

Ed called. Months back, some driver
                too at ease with ice
had picked him off, let others
                pick him up. Blank
— careful as if they called from
                the surface still, "Ed...
Hey, Ed," he didn't want the whole

way back yet. That
helped earth our spaces. There were
                    stars anyway about to leap
from the screen of their own good looks
                    to eat us up. And then one
day of thaw, an hour on the horizon
                    a band of red played,
brass yellowing sky's blown everything.

Driving The Snowy River

It was over, the goodwill season, and even
our tree still switched on in hopes of a second
coming was snuffed by the light of day.
Decorations hung around asking too much.
Why not just write cheques, advised my poems.

Dwindling out of the distance, Jeff called
with that smile on a tight leash. Was it
his job at the bank, some shadow he was born in?
Robust, eating as she drove, maybe Beth
had convinced him life wasn't his natural element.

The river's snow dome swirled.
Trees like ropes strung from branches
striped both banks plumping for low profiles
that panes of ice slid past unbroken.
Against the current, gulls could hang-glide.

Persuading boulders to inch further,
the river surged and though in branched shadow
not one stone seemed to move,
in Utah Lake whole mountains would see
themselves, the art all art thirsts to mirror.

At the bridge when I glanced back,
drifts switched to running my way.
Then trees gave way to hills. Sky rose.
Eyes flew straight where the reeds sighed
over vanishing perspectives, a heron

staring fish into its radius pinioned the lake,
and though even this new season creaked
shining skated me on as if everything
was crushed into one small part of the country
white and only once, this once.

Weeks later, I left the car that had just ridden
rocks into the canyon. Climbed with my wife,
daughter, breathing, and in skidmarked snow
we stopped for our lives to catch us up.
The bent road was going straight

now we'd rebounded, floating on thin air.
Drivers stopped, spoke urgent smoke
but police knew the accidenting season:
welcome back, lucky the river's low.
Home later, why should I stop talking?

Lights at the sharp edge of expectation
coming on like fires burned dinner plates
white, print swerved as a newspaper shook my hand.
On the sports channel: bodybuilders.
My eyes headed south from bunched shoulders

through valleys of the bicep, outcrops
of scalloped leg. When I turned in bed,
strange how my stomach arrived late.
Time for self-discipline, I swore,
self-everything, then failed to sleep.

Next day, remembered musclemen like pet shops
twitched and wriggled. Wife, daughter, offered
selfscapes in proportion. Things levelled off.
But as if to prove heights gained are only canyons
upside down, now the lights came on like lights.

Snow Rats

Thinking of Idaho, the sky fluttered its dark-browed paleness shut,
heavy with plans, but settled on us. Morning wore afternoon.
We eased out on a crust of light already bushes had grown through,
floating our footprints, pleased with the fat sky sprawled replete.
What to do with it, stare? Not enough, my daughter thought,
nudging from sloth a fluffed plumpness weather sends
for reawakenings. Spades scraped emerald arcs around a tumbledome.

That winter, too, in the river opposite I drowned her pet rat's
ratlets, raw squirming thumbs in a plastic bag. Try stroking Silky,
she'd say, pointing its mad electric head. It hopped humpbacked,
chased by a tail like a fast intestine. My lamplight's circle
shrank. Once when it frisked my leg I yelled, shook her like —

For her, the dome was a kneeling someone to be coaxed or patted up
with promises of buttons, a head. Pride in our created self
lasted two, at most three days then arms slumped in accelerated age.
Eyes sank. In a drained landscape though, fading slowest: the man
gathered from cold, something newmade that is the last to go.

Muskrats meanwhile, whiskery bachelors wedded to prim standards,
parted the river when they dived. One sat washing.
She longed to take it home and at that range, well, I could see
her point. She and water took so much in their stride.
Down the river's slide, muskrats on business surfaced not just
in my head and, with her rat at home, it seemed best
(though I never got too close) to go with the flow of her.

Natural History

Of seven men propping up their ease,
some wear boaters in what seems
a wooden cage. The camera stares back.
Surrounded: a gaze roped to a sturdy
crossbeam. It drops through the floor
from long black glistening hair, a pelt.

And here's another photo, passenger pigeons,
flights towards eclipse. Who'd guess they could
be plucked from loaded trees by torchlight?
One tethered pigeon, its eyes sewn,
flapping, would call thousands to the nets.
Pigs grew fat on the thudding young.
Then there was a whirring of concern
and the last lived till 1914 at Cincinnati Zoo.

Glance back again, nothing has changed.
New in the sun, the structure supporting them
is white except where a shadow falls down stairs
to *The hanging of Firamini the Papago Indian.*
Almost suspended animation. Since the trapdoor
hasn't opened yet, he keeps an upright patience.

Stillwater Blues

We were in the high school band.
I was lead clarinet and he was popular, high
on the fancy outfit, blue with broad gold stripes.
For Don Horowitz nothing second-hand,

guns especially, his dad knew
how to hunt. "It's a real nice day, Don," Mrs. Timms
the doctor's wife said once. "Why don't you
go and kill something?" He did too,

blank sense of humour, charm
fully loaded. When he came home that time, one
of the Few Good Men the Marines dressed fit to kill,
girls waved. He was aimed at Vietnam

the year we built the shopping mart
outside of Stillwater, keeping Dad's business going
when the town was all but dead. Who could tell
things over there would fall apart?

He just dumped himself
is how my father said it. Doped-up in his trailer
a year on, Don sat in overalls, slippers,
on a car seat — a shelf

for all that I could say
to talk him down — staring out everything.
Then he left town jobless and I haven't seen him
since. Until today.

He's killed a man, Don Horowitz.
I see in the *Star* he's Donald Furness now. In the photo,
dazed, he's looking for, what, a job, name (something
beyond him anyway that fits),

and they say he tried to unmake
what this country made of him, threw it all away.
No law against that, feel sorry for him. But hell,
you got to pay for your mistakes.

Motel

I got the key
then climbed the metal stairs.

When I opened the door
there was a woman, two small boys.
She asked what had taken
me so long and had I phoned yet.
The two boys
turned back to their tv.

We've been together years.
What if, I wonder sometimes,
I'd opened some other door?

Say Hello To Phoenix

(for Song Ho)

1. our lights beat their white wings
   and landed free. cheerfully I greet relatives.

   now is all. buildings have no shadows.

   the Old Man one night near death
   he said What should I be thinking.
   now is here in a suit.

   so many cars. night's driving
   flak that won't burn out. hair of relatives
   on fire — look back and what am I expecting.
    maybe water so calm
    its banks fall through the sky.

   once near Tay Ninh I fished clouds.

   we stop. burnt charcoal after flares.
   now the moon is newcomer too hello
   Moon I am from HochiMinh city.

2. My niece is a bird, get up
   and go. I clean house.
   When she enters,
   my heart stands up.
   Her big American
   makes coffee like ashes.
   One day in the garage wrapped
   in white sheets,
   he was spattered red like the car.
   I said no, no, walked away.

3. I think going measures what returning
    is for, though there is no returning.
    Where are the walkers, old people?
    This is a long street running away.
    When planes come I look up
    and am not here, a head floating.

    I write poems again after work.
    Not storage, remaking, the better rescue
    best if, look, no hands.
    Sometimes there are letters waiting
    with the thought of rain
    but hummingbirds spin and I praise this other
    life that flies through to outlast us.

Catfish

We arrived late. He was a friend's uncle, a name
given to spare us one motel, unlucky streaks
of freeway, whose planks leaned on his shack's
wit's end. From a grey head, eyes
gripped where they landed. We answered
in loud British, thrown by his bucking twang.

Just him left with three rooms of the farm grown up
and gone. Work overalls were slumped from a nail
like a taller man, things ploughed and scattered
belonged if they could just remember how.
Supper. He'd be moved soon to the city.
Curtains breathed green as a car unzipped the dark.

Next day, early, when we couldn't see for sun
the smokestacks up ahead, flakes in the shuffle
gleamed as trees panned light. Odd
he'd want us to take his photo. And that catfish
he cooked — we'd watched its mouth open and close
and open how long after the body had been cut off?

Freedom Boulevard

My daughter talked namebrand jeans, the Mall,
as we left the city on 200 West that became one day
without a blush Freedom Boulevard. Bulging in heat,
cars wobbled like toads. Each day she chants in class,
"I pledge allegiance to the flag of the United States..."

The road racing straight ahead, uncoiling sun,
braked in the mining district. You climb past Ephraim
into Wales from the east and it's small,
dry ground's shrunk to a litter of bleached jobs.
Turkey sheds glared into gaps left unexplained.
At the tiny post office, when Mary Davis scanning
my postcard asked if that's Welsh, "No, that's
my writing," I said. Keep Off signs peppered testily
with buckshot said connection is accident, that's all.

Sight's longer in dry air: weightless, we fell
like stones on distance whose ripplings
smoothed themselves to a circle with no edges,
the one target that proves anyone's aim true.

The drive-in had *Snow White.* Desert had the darkness,
even the flagged principalities of car dealerships.
Where our block squared its shoulders, the garage
yawned surprise — isn't the point of travel to keep
going? — then shut up.

Country

Roaming the airwaves again are rhinestone
cowgirls called Tammy, Loretta, Crystal,
with doomwails of steel guitars.
My wipers blink the blurred road
clear. Even the river nursed in its bed
by sympathetic branches lends an ear.

Heart-stomped, they're stranded
in love's garden. Why though pick late-flowering
philanderers? To be on their wavelength,
I'd need me a Ford pickup and more.
Folk I was raised with kept their griefs
well under wraps, they had no truck
with breakdowns. Would they be leaning on hard
shoulders here, mourning the humped bridge?

But trying to switch off,
my arm does the hesitation waltz.
"Ease up," soft tyres sigh.
"Let go, let go," whisper wipers.

Hymns used to work for them. No road though
runs back, and anyway the songs
aren't all strife. Why not just sag along?
This one's all heart, listen, *Dropkick Me
Jesus Through the Goalposts of Life.*

Independence

Drugs, promiscuity,
unscriptured sickness spreads.
When I saw Luther King
in their textbook, I pulled
the kids from school
and that triggered it,
that with the other trouble.

We got a life here, four of us,
three acres. Water gets stolen though,
you got to check the flow.
Not many places left. McCabe's.
Dent's. Land uses people up.

When cops came to the gate,
I'd nailed a message:
We the people on this property
are a Nation under God
INDEPENDENT AND SEPARATE.

A big electronic message board
flashed. I replied, morse code
with a mirror, "Cops not telling truth".

At night, banks of floodlights,
and highpitched noise
till I shot the speakers out.
We've set trip wires,
hung fish hooks at eye level.

Kay has the binoculars.
I say to Kay, nine days
and they're getting nowhere.
The kids are cooking fritos.

Those who come against
this my people
will verily be destroyed.

Utah

Nudged, sprinklers woke sneezing
on green outposts dry again,
arms flung against morning
heat that slipped through airily. Rains
arced and fanned, sprayed beads,
splinters of burst light, falls
splashing empty streets all mine.
Plants were drunk as seaweed.
But heat bulged and, by midday, on walls
webs of water hadn't survived its shine.

Fat nights later, I wandered
between lamp islands. A flare. Splayed
branches in distress. It hovered,
flaunting a scorched roof, then blazed
as I skeltered, banged the door, scuffed
words into the man half-naked faced
with night and what water's for.
One stream was not enough.
Fire trucks were. I'd traced
what seemed street theatre —

but had glimpsed what the open door
had opened. A curled room: two children
drowse for another second under roars
reddening the attic's den.
Toys spread around. Sparked, a man dives
to aim hosed sprawls
as his wife wading through delirium
runs to evacuate their lives.
Later, I thought of my wife, daughter, all
of us under what heat might come,

and saw the infinite desert reach
past scoured ribs of ghost towns
way back and beyond to breeched
defences, ways of living blown.
Sage brush spikes its boundaries
but this town endures. In channels,
more than pumped water gathers streets.
Rippling, its surge frees
lives for the sharing, holds lines
green, intact in the face of heat.

Losing Ground

He's going, the phonecall said. A mind
that paced dictionaries of late, inclined
to rising ground, then slowed to his shuffling
has stopped almost. Easy to imagine
not take in. That cragged mafioso face:
little there will be displaced.
Jarred by so small a claim, sightings
unconfirmed but eager to be insights
drift like smoke on just-crossed terrain.
Find anything? they signal. *You'll not be here again.*

He taught Latin, watched words retreat
as cold print itself dragged overtaken feet,
sat firm in his chapel's drawn-out
last stand, advanced a family. Without
much liking the town, a tourist bedspread,
he lumped that wittily too. He kept his head
a fort, looked to the unchanged sea.
And, Mr. Hughes, father-in-law, was gruffly kind to me.
I'm at a loss. So memory trails
this wide. Taking refuge from, or seeking, detail?

Little comes anyway. Clipped hedging in place
of openings, here a blur, there just traces...
Much the same when, lazy-timid,
I first baulked at it — or what it hid.
Such short patrols we made on either side
in an evergreen reserve. Reasonable guides,
they should have helped in the long run, what and why,
so loss as when my father died,
jerked, doubles in pain:
No, no, another chance, let's try again.

At Spanish Fork

Under the trees,
familiar names are mustered.
In families still,
hauled overland, words

measuring distance say
there's no way back again.
Most who climbed
mountains found the plain —

West was a verb. Dank
half-remembered streets
it buried in shine. And some
collided with strange heat

like the grandson of Evan
Evans whose sandstone psalm
is blurred: James Allen Evans
d. 1970 U.S. Army Vietnam.

Mormons

Roads under snapped peaks have eased us
from towns so small their children
glanced up. Sidetracked history rusts cars.
The sun's trailed us through conditioned air
so even from Emigration Canyon
focal points relate: steeples lift
the plain. The faith not ours, ways
people with our names helped make
glint at desert. Salt Lake City

is a landing place. Those faceless
facing walls: when a big wind shook them,
yes they said to voices calling Jump
that gave them first the Atlantic,
yes to cholera, the Mississippi ocean,
waggons inched a thousand miles into space
under weather's gritted teeth. All slipped land
theirs not their own. And, faith wrapped
around them, keeping the desert out,

received this land. Blown to another world
on prayers, first they had to make it,
the sky striped red then stars flying.
Proposed: we should build as a nation
along the Jordan River with Elizabeth Lewis
as queen. Rejected. But though parched —
two climates merging, heat drains
moisture almost memory — a New Wales breathed.
Sun blinked at the Spanish Fork eisteddfod.

At the university they helped build
are few who can translate them.
Their great-grandchildren who know London
do not know each other. Flight paths converge,
fade out, as sky measures gain and loss.
And soon, welcome as coming here,
our return will give us cloud country again,
pierced by what's beyond, that must keep
changing and not changing to stay intact.

Soft Times

Pick, shovel, swinging from bent knees
slack now from après-ski

in bars just bright enough
to know smooth money likes a bit of rough,

forging a career in boutiques
where a day's work takes all week,

once this was a mining town. Light suits
glide around on cowboy boots.

Park City, a gallery yawns. Lamps haunt
an antique shop or seance

(much polished, there's a tommy box)
and someone's selling rocks.

Downvalley, soft on the prowl
from hotels padded out like jowls,

fish tamers near grassed-over tips
crack soundless whips.

Scale the main street, older
now breath's a parrot on your shoulder.

Unnatural, you squawk. *What's been purposeful
shouldn't lounge all cash and bull,*

then think how admiring parents saw you, how
your child must see you now.

11.

Tracks

(for Derek Richardson)

Cloud-skimming where wheels can choose
just routes, dust shrugs off fences,
roads, as the Utah desert comes to town.
At night a river spills over, murmuring Why not?
People dream it into their lives by different
names. In antlered garages, faithful pickups wait
to force back the horizon, shoulders rolling,
making off with the roads. A place of sense
may need for clear sight short tenancies.

Over here? replies Holywell. It's ruins
have most space to accommodate what we bring them.
Mill walls stretch, patched green, in search of
something to enclose where children threaded
on stiff workrates were once profit's dangled bait.
Here, now, lives that made arrivals of both
converge with new lives at such junctions.
Though words have soared from the moon,
our true trajectories do not end in space,

Between two worlds, the signalman scans the town.
His window's still flecked with blackout paint.
Inland, rooms fondling tv, is the streets' stopped
slide down to hearths two centuries cold. But he
turns and standstill's cover's blown where sea
scrapes distance clear so the mute tide, plunging,
detonates with one surge what the other has given.
He lives on lines leaning in then out, gleams
of tall ladders you want to climb both ways.

Burying The Waste

(Holywell)

Trapped by Caradoc, favourite of a king,
even Winifred could not deny his sword.
Where hair leaked blood, a well of healing
sprang, then the stream hurrying its hoard
of news woke up the valley. Winifred
drew pilgrims limping, eager to be whole.
He signed up slaves of cotton, copper, lead.
Her stream, severed by water wheels, rolled
machines. When Winifred spread her arms wide
to make from shadows trees, he cut them down
but she thinned the Dee channel. Its quayside
became silent, the valley a ghost town.
Now buildings sprawl headless. All around,
sprung green, half-buried: still misshapen ground.

*

Not just the Church preferred its blessings high.
This cotton mill snatched six storeys of sky
with stone from the nearby abbey's shell
then, power untapped, St. Winifred's Well.
An act of God, a world in seventy days.
High too squire Pennant's recorded praise:
all the workers flourished, dined on meat,
fish, "in commodious houses". Work was sweet.

Poet Jones of Llanasa, muffled voice
of the backwater — why couldn't he rejoice?
"Rods doom'd to bruise in barb'rous dens of noise
the tender forms of orphan girls and boys."
Poets. They build nothing. Just hover, stare,
write maudlin history. Except he'd worked there.

Ingenuity flowers in such fumes.
New copper bolts were roots helping great ships
spread wide. Brass beakers moistening the lips
of Africa, exchanged for slaves, seemed blooms.

Up there, notice, a fly-wheel gouged the wall.
In this bank, too, an opening faced with brick
like an oven gone drowsily rustic;
no grass, webs or wormcasts though. Earth, that's all

almost. Hereabouts being where the knack
of refining human brushes took hold —
twigs bound in rags who carefuly swept back
arsenic from this flue and lived to rot —
last year they found a skull, some ten-year-old
ingenuity planted then forgot.

*

The wall keeps on haemorraging dark green
through the bricked-up centuries, through soil
Meadow Mill injected with copper spoil.
And its damp spillway is coloured gangrene
in memory of times, as Pennant said,
when workers obeyed the "antient law"
of sluicing thoroughly before meals or
watched "eruptions of a green colour" spread.
(They knew dogs, if they licked the sheeting, slept
for good.) So justice as well, urbane,
copper-bottomed, is remembered here. Yet
though the wall's washed scrupulously by rain,
strange that metal still heaves through. Dogs drop.
It has tasted men and starves and cannot stop.

For three years, Frederick Rolfe alias
Baron Corvo, the Crow, pecked at the shell
of Holywell. He saw in it himself,
more idea than place, a proud man mostly
beak who squabbled, wrote and painted, furious
with "Sewer's End", obscurity's rebel
till fury grew him wings. Two crows he left
in painted banners still caw "Look at me!"

Flashing, art's narrowed gaze will open
on polluted water and turn even stones
to mirrors. The Well running wheels ran men.
Its stream's "uproll and downcarol" Manley
Hopkins sang rang walls from where Poet Jones,
apprenticed to heartache, jumped to sea.

*

Ice tore a trench to the estuary.
Grass healed its sides. Water devised a well.
An idea, grown around it like a tree
surviving as an arched stone spell,
towered so pilgrims are still beckoned here,
a welling of belief that named a town.
When another idea for water
bricked up the flow, its weight wore people down.

The centuries keep waking to change dreams.
Dug from the undergrowth: brickwork's feud
with stone for possession of the stream.

And voices insisting water is alive —
those pursuing always and, pursued,
those in need of miracles to survive.

Visiting George

They don't help much, he seems to think,
pursed jowls, concern on stalks. "Do you
remember...?" He doesn't: he'd stood with a grasp
of phrases in his teeth. Then his tongue was there
locked, and he wasn't standing. Slow-lidded
eyes check which effort might call first.

Poured on a small screen, showbiz fizzes.
Will he ask who the rakish Someone is,
selling his new something, bounced off the latest
chat show to this ward? No. Ex-miner, his own light
tilts his head. From here he can see the trees
where flatness holds what watersheds let go.

Back home, that cosh he liberated from a guard
creaks a language living rooms don't speak.
With an ambulance brigade, mouth covered, cloth
disinfectant-soaked, once at a German camp
he saw the known world end but would not talk
of this. "Don't say I can't," he'd tell his kids.

So visiting's over. Past trees inching up to green,
Closed signs face permanence, leather jackets keen
on openings. From lanes, the road gathers,
ready to skate way out, trusting in length and luck.
All seems a pause like that note in the camp
diary his son mentioned: "Nobody died today".

Downing

Seventy, rasping, he lives in the saddlery
of the estate now run out of paths.
He keeps the tv. busy. The past? The brisk squire
who toured the eighteenth century and met Voltaire?
Not interested. But around pleasure garden, summer house,
Bob Weston cleared gullies for parched ironworks,
lopped trees in the dingles, was tolerant it seems
of poachers. The house, burned down as an insurance job,
is a DIY kit. Its drive can't find the gateway.
Tunnels though and waterways built by miners
are intact, theirs or land's revenge on stateliness
where ponds sag under weed.

Below on Mostyn sands, cockles have been found
by diggers in balaclavas linked to the underground economy.
Jobs, they're rare as oysters. Unmarked trucks
sidled, and from dunes, they say, the DHSS took photos.
Bob Weston's watched — Dunkirk again, another
scramble, grab what you can then home, the brass
will know the score. Except the brass aren't on your side.

Now that it's wanted for caravans, what no one could visit
is lamented. People will flood in, there'll be petitions.
But he'll not be collecting who likes that brandnew
pub at the junction and leaves his dog at home.

Starting Point

Where you started from didn't stop because you left.
Well, no. Hard though to take unflinching
new kinds of doubt you were ever there.
Since the station slumped beyond rescue
way past rails, the river's hauled no hardware.
In clean water, rust keeps coming through.

Expecting patronage — the child you were
the place seemed too, elsewhere made you adult —
it covers tracks, blurs highlights, spreads.
Still, leaves in the playground jump. Sheds leaning
on back lanes forgot to change. Both parents dead,
what but those streets know who you've been?

Once left, the starting place goes soon,
arrives where the road that shrugged you off
chose what's now resolutely called home.
And called home is what you are when slopes pause
for slate roofs to slice a river. Or say honeycombed
workings sag — it's as if new accents echoed yours.

Anywhere, anyway, terraced houses glimpsed
bring in that hill you mean to cross before
it's too late. For difference haunts too, offering
another self to visit, at least a different slant.
But there's a tug. You keep on looking back. Nothing
almost. You were never meant to leave and can't.

Sunday Fishing

Dunes strumming high thin tunes
drift off. Clouds bounce
on water. You could build a sky
where, aimed arches, walls
from their own burstings rise.
But now sea's tied a length
of men to itself and sprawls,
watching them reel in lines
it slackens then retrieves in arcs:
sand-sharp, its edge shines

rays of spool. Sea gleams
at its own snatchings
until all lines are taut.
And the men, determined —
rods, eyes, hopes, caught
on baited waves — are another line
unbroken. Voices swirl in wind.
Spray's banter is answered.
Tightening the men, a current
runs between them stirred

by what absorbs them,
slow rollers folding over,
drowning out pale lives
awash with the news, how
only the ringing Now survives
even light's levering itself
back down to dusk, Now
in the tide's carillon again,
on a dwindling beach
where the sea is fishing men.

The Beach

My son: eight years old so he ran
　　full sail to clear glass, black glass
　　smashed, swept back powdered.
　　Two shells I pocketed, white, ribbed
　　like bootprints they'd survived.
　　I watched him testing distance.
　　He'd turn, still checking
　　his trail would be mine. Wind that
　　gusts things in and blows things out
　　threw voices at my head. I kept also
　　a bird's skull whitening.

My father collected money, friends.
　　Since he died I've worn his coat.
　　His jangling coins in the lining
　　I can't reach insist
　　it doesn't fit　it doesn't fit.
　　At night when the town went out
　　water slipped in. I took it
　　in my head to be a cellar.

My wife mocked my "loose ends".
　　All my pieces, dry, rubbed white,
　　I've stored in my chest — bleached
　　rope, a knot only I can untie.
　　Shells, driftbones. I know
　　their meanings and, fool, told them.

My chest I hid then.
  They wanted what I've got
  my wife who set
  the boy prying I never
  meant to harm.
  But I was right they
  came and brought me here
  new faces questions

  a good white cleanness though

  tonight she will not visit
  again but the chest's safe.

Wings

Time hadn't mattered till her husband's ran out.
The house, spreading, made an evening of itself.
Reedy flats stretching out to a horse
and banging door for company met roofs on the run
from dunes. Careful, afternoons measured
the estuary where tides weighed logs
then put them down, where hours drowned like clouds.

When the ex-minister, fifties like her, kept calling,
his beard through pipesmoke she read first
as contentment. He had seen the world and shrugged.
Wrong, he had dabbled in property till it bit him.
He'd collect firewood, taking logs for a stroll
in a stripped pram, put up coveys of gulls
brought down as he tracked the shoreline. She saw
not washed-up footprints, water quicken slippery
as wind past the lighthouse, rippling implications.
Ships had been juggled long distance till its arms shrank.

The roof leaked. Mornings he'd spread planks, tools
and disappear. He'd finished the process
of getting started. And would have finished
the job but then the roofing season ended.

Once at dusk when she'd thrown stale bread,
the window floating, floating with white wings
settled on water. Not just perspective though
of the opposite shore kept sea dreams in check.
He wanted to preach again so she fixed up
practices at Bethel, listened from empty pews
and drove him home. Theirs was an oldish house.
The roof seemed shaky but faith might hold it up.

Decoys

My timber for carving's from the shore,
driftlumps water sluices out
so it dries fast and won't crack. Elm most of all.
Bones in the woodshed's drought,
they clench. Opened months later, a store
of ripeness surprised is the windfall.

We'd leave for Mostyn, cross
the Shrouds. You had to know the water.
What use is a duck-punt once a week?
You're not informed. Birds on the ebb won't stir,
just sit there packed. The flood brings chaos.
High tide meant hide-and-seek.

I carve birds, ducks often: pintail
and mallard, a teal, shapes wood lays for the hand.
Bandsaw for roughing out — check the grain
runs with the bill. Chisels, rasp. Elm is hard sand.
With oil or polish, what's been fingered stale,
another late surprise, is sunburnt terrain.

Each day — start early. We liked a NE
in the face when we picked our spot:
no wobblings, steady as she... Sixty yards
for a clean kill. 20 ounces. AA shot.
But for food, I wouldn't have killed — at least
not birds. Smooth the feathers, keep no scorecard.

Best I like the curve where crown, cheek,
sweep down through the swell of chest,
the sweptback, cleared-for-action prow
of a poised gathering unrest
that, from the moment's peak,
though wood, might just take off, go anyhow.

It wasn't the birds mainly,
that's something I can't nail.
One chap I took, a February morning,
sang for hours — threats to shoot him failed.
Never sung before. The estuary
was fine, I lived on dusk and dawn.

Beyond wood: an airy something
from nothing wood's a pretext for.
Alone at last with the whole mind's scope,
you drift. Almost a familiar shore.
Stirrings, gleams are stalked, and springing
this time they are yours, you hope.

Things To Do When The Town's Closed

Our choir dressed as guerrilla butlers
has driven the holidaymakers back.
It is September. Seagulls
are critics prying over spilt ink.
The town's scraped off its silver lining
to get at the cloud instead.

In search of a bit of life,
Ron has started taxidermy, juggling
bags of skin like a homicidal vet.
They grin from furry cells,
near-squirrels.
You can't keep a good man up.

And Mr. S has emptied his firm's safe.
Self-bloodied, he faked
assault then described the villain
so well for the police photofit,
like a shout his own face rang out.

On the library wall: *ANACKY*.
Draughts from the Mersey Tunnel quicken
across the Dee. Wait,
slow down
at the station.
You can find yourself elsewhere.

Balloons were released in August
from Ffrith Beach for Holiday Fun
with addressed labels. W's returned
all the way from Builth. His prize?
First cash, soon a court appearance:
winds blew north that day so how come W's balloon
went south? Well, live in town
and wind is just a ghost. The label went
via his aunt in Builth, both ways by post.

Yesterday, high on a ladder with acres
to paint, Mr. S was whistling 'Born Free'.
And although the Pleasant Sunday Afternoon Society
now meets all week, although the slipper women
at the laundrette seem lively
and waves roll up in fits watching dunes
fail to outwit caravans,
it's a bad time.

We are alone together.
Even our jeweller's stopped twinkling.
You can't help but feel
someone out there might be planning chainsaw
psychiatry or florist pressing.

Scenes From The Age Of Marvels

The giant claw
        squats in dim living rooms
        flickering, gently tears off
        flakes of lives still warm,
        and each room tells the same story.

Blodeuwedd is changed into an owl:
        Here's a woman selling carpets.
        Here is a man baring teeth.
        Pinned, Blod hears
        of the one known cure for stains
        while out in the park
        wire has one thousand wings
        and zebras grazing in sunlight
        turn into benches.

Lleu in the form of an eagle
        has come to a screeching stop
        in almost — Los Angeles.
        About to swoop from his Mustang,
        gun in his good right hand,
        and smear some sidewalk punk, he turns
        when Blod passes him a cup.
        Fatal — shot clean through his cardi.
        She sips her tea.

Rhiannon on a magic horse:
        She's had enough.
        Ben watches one side
        and videos another,
        a life in vibrant
        aspic. It's over.
        Now watch her vanishing tr —

The Leaning Tree

It's the annual Welsh play, our daughter has a line.
In the hall, crowded, warm not stuffy, where faces
moon backstage, Miss Evans' set wins oscars:
a tree on a manic heath leans out of puff
like a stricken witch. Lights out at last, and silence.

This time I get the plot (translated) not the point.
A warning about marriage? Folk tales dig deep —
simply through having been here once already,
the past's wiser. I wish I could grasp its drift.
It drifts as I sink, my clothes a nest...

        ...Since the Roman remains were uncovered,
for instance, things have been different in town.
Shoulders and roads have straightened. White apron slung
over one shoulder, the fishmonger harangues us,
mornings bring thunderous claps of mail. Our mayor

would have retaken Gaul but for problems with his family.
They want to kill him. Newly important, the Vicar juggling
squirrels' entrails flings an arm at the sun. What could
we do without him? Omens are good. Phalanxes and columns,
 sponsored, are on the move at —

Applause. I'm stormed alert. Cups of tea sweeten
Mr. Williams' proud speech, next the cast is here.
"How old is Smoky," she asks excited (though not of me),
"and what's *needless to say* in Welsh?" "You were very
very good," I say. Sometimes even things I missed seem clear.

Farmland

Inland from the English-speaking sea,
where I lose my bearings and my wife translates,
market towns gather villages.
Henllan, Trefnant, Llanrhaeadr had come
past trees brushing mist from the fields
to Denbigh's plantation of telegraph poles.

Steps stood up, and high arched doors
checking again familiar faces
narrowly took me in. On her aunt's
coffin, flowers had drained the light
but not those packed pews: murmurs, ripples
were refilling farmland's hollows.

The minister's shock of eyebrows
hedging raw cheeks, he'd have hauled a ram.
Speech shook me off. It was tenors
gliding on familiar foreign words in search
of thermals drew me towards the woman
gone, to Joe who doesn't speak Welsh

or often, relying on closed ranks.
Once connection tunes its instruments,
feeling's airborne over fact
and, soaring, forgets it still bears
language asserting difference, how else
leap snags of common ground?

At the coast were fingers of cloud
all bruises and gold rings. Caravans
made one thin road an anywhere.
What we travel from also moves from us,
and gulls guarding clutches of pebbles
turned into people briefly then flew off.

North

There's lead in the ground: sweat down this shaft
became ore then memorial damp. Crevices chew ferns.
In the cave, fanned branches flickering
scrawl on the walls where stones grind underfoot.
Passages, whichever way they point, lead back.

Even winter hasn't cleared a path uphill
to packets, tins, he's hung from trees
rattling out his territory. His place is a shell.
Mats of cracked slate glint if the sky's switched on,
also a mound of rubbish. Hoarse branches seem at home.

Was that him by the road, sighting along a stick
Pow! Pow! at crows? At the hospital, thickset
like an old coat stuffed with bracken, someone lurched
from a lift to a board blaring ward names, offices
and the message *You Are Here.* But he was not.

Since limestone hoards water thirstily,
the stream's trailed all the way by trees which can
stand stockstill. The loud coast sends its probes inland.
As if he's learned how to live listening at crevices,
he moves in an absence, and visitors never arrive.

But advancing flatness wants high ground. Miles west,
calling, they climb. No answer — just trickles of slate,
water's white fingers slipping. They're not fooled:
they trace shelters, angles slabbed against rain.
And houses are checked, those roofed especially,

part-ruins look near-built. Everywhere, footprints.
They scrawl messages in the wrong language,
leave food scraps, different groups each time.
Through quarries, paths haul slate. Gates promise
something worth opening up. So much going on

sharpens what isn't. The roof having fallen
on Tanygrisiau which once called people
to mornings snapped awake, loss calls on loss.
Each summer among rubble, why else would they come?
They won't give up. Nothing is ever over.

On A Portrait By Kyffin Williams

A country near-slouch has spread
his knees. In the background
gone blank, a tousled shadow lives.
And somewhere a shadow jet, gorse
its escort of yellow pennants.

Though the chin has rounded on
its youth, like water he could get
up and stretch and walk across country.
High in the drowned valley,
conifers meet mirror selves.

His brown face weather-veined,
ready to answer, gleams
for a self not yet rubbed smooth —
somewhere he'd know, burnt roofs send up
the price of occupation.

Eyes aren't sure what they feel
about this. Such hair though
it must take shears to tame. One hand
clamps a knee to earth, the other
lifts like a big cup his busby.

The hall is still tonight.
He is at ease but not wholly
perhaps, Corporal Pritchard, Goat Major,
in red and gold, the uniform
weight of our country's two colours.

Translations

In Llyn, light's starved the hills
to mist, brought treetops down.
Winter regroups — and on.
The lane knows where the gate is.
Now ranked slate and marble
straighten the way and all belongs
with ribs of wall, bleached fields,

till a straggle of wooden crosses
makes for the trees, reaches
grass, the new diggings, not
the fence. Lives shaken loose
unfinished frenzy scattered.
Where is secured ground?
Last shakings spread them here.

There was help, the roof held.
Stranded, still at the camp, the old
write *Polska 19 — Penrhos, Walia 19 —*
for the dead. Stormed ground
has known enough about retreat
to take them in; fields
hush what they knew of earth.

If not in Krakow or Brodach,
these could be crossing some city
square of ours they'd exile
from forgetfulness, where Paulina
Wasilewska's *Pros! O Modlitwe,*
Please Pray For Me, would speak
not just to nodding grass.

But it's quiet, the trees
are just this side of silence.
And death needs that at least
to translate into different
languages even words it knows
by heart: *You are we. We are you.*
We are the same people.

Dic Aberdaron

So he went looking.
Languages are other words
to live in, but that wasn't it.

Grown tall on vocabularies,
soon he could look over hedges,
people. Stature wasn't it.

He'd open another road — to Athens,
say, and read himself there —
though place wasn't it.

He was a beard walking barefoot,
a coat of many pages. People
watched. Pathetic, wasn't...?

It took their whole lives'
weight to stop them finding
searching and not finding it was it.

Seeking Them Out

1.

Feet track their lost holidays
through Boots, the castle, Boots,
marching up and down. Froth-moustached,
pebbles click wrinkled heels.
But west is another country.

The far walls, step by step,
relive their hoisting uphill;
they're full of gaps now, a lot's
slipped through. Maybe
west, which is another...

With high new sails, hills are leaving
accommodations for home truths
as slopes send down scree to pierce
the running fence. West —
west is the idea of Patagonia.

2.

Across the sea, from a shimmer
under the Shining Mountains: news.
A white-skinned tribe, coracles, hill-forts —
"one branch of the Welsh nation
has preserved its independence to this day".

Preparing to seek them out,
Iolo Morgannwg lives in the woods
rough with his language and theirs.
Berries are sweet, old metres new.
In the tree of Wales, a spirit army sings
so sharp it cuts the wind.

Ready to seek them out, his friend
John Evans' ship is tugged to America.
Upriver he toils to the new world's rim.
And though "I am able to inform you
that there is no such people
as the Welsh Indians", truth
and belief are different valleys.

Between them: the lit peak, Y Wladfa.
Paths clambering pause, regroup, arc
to Patagonia, newfoundland of the spirit.

3.

June, 1982. At Government House, the crockery's
intact but, weeks back, its flag changed colour.
Now Stanley is Puerto Argentino.

Milton-Rees from Patagonia, NCO
and secretary with three languages, replaces
the madonna on his general's desk.
It is winter. He is not thinking of Trelew.
From San Carlos, the British have marched
so fast through the mountains, why,
General Menéndez, still look out to sea?
Yesterday the police station was hit.
In Buenos Aires, they worry about football.

Between shellbursts, wind sings so sharp
it has long since flattened trees,
scouring gun positions, trenches.
Men unravel through red alerts.
Near the waterfront, hulks chainsawn
for firewood sink in the conscripts' stoves.
Some, disembarked from the *Bahia Paraiso*,
can speak Welsh like Milton-Rees.

Others prepare to seek them out.
It is morning, the end of a long journey.
Sir Galahad won't reach Bluff Cove.

Ffestiniog

(for David Nash, sculptor)

What to do with a chapel
tossed on broken slate
but buoy it up
with beech, chestnut,
that have floating to do
shaping their arrivals?

Boats leaping through prows
make their own waves,
rough-hewn close up.
At a distance, since
chestnut's learned its cleaving,
eyes skim under way.

Curved outlines, stirring,
wood's left in midair.
Foal is a foal-shaped space
in a mare of sycamore that
won't forget, her offspring
beside her, sprung.

What to do
with a cleft in the hills
slate-stopped?
Open it, open it, make
a mouth wood sings through,
relearning celebration.

Barry John

who tacked like a yacht
through breakers,
tidewreck where he'd

been, whose arms, hips,
swapped fly half
— truths tacklers grasped

too late, was a spool
casually unwound
around sharp eyes

lining him up just right.
Then he'd crossed
their lines, parachuted

in, pass master
of the national art,
straightforward veering.

Bards

At the Caerwys eisteddfod of 1568, a permit system
sought to distinguish genuine poets from the rest.
Licence applicants were judged by experts.

Northward they flew, flushed warblers,
waves of wordsmiths in a whirr
much vaunted, pally valour
plumed in a valley pallor.
Some were skylarks, some thickskinned
parrots on a palsied wind.

Starred high fliers, hawks of sense,
were launched on poetic licence
but most raved at rejection's slip,
with tumbled owls found kinship.
Showbirds in dylanesquish fits
rewarmed scrambled eggs of wit;
doves of peace with sharp beaks,
hair-breasted, brandished leeks.
Bards sat slurring whole sestets
of bitter and sounding wet,
freethinkers with three thoughts —
then they dived south distraught
under poetry's bright shield:
egoes rampant on a brazen field.

Stern Caerwys, true arts council,
steel in the memory still.
You cleared from the land its host
of cuckoos for ever almost,
and two large truths you left us.
It's a long haul to Parnassus.
Most of us winged by words
are essentially home birds.

Flight Patterns

Staying, moving. Both versions
claim the coast, illusions

of choice steep
depths here and beyond keep

prompting: packed in redoubts,
hiders watch runners wearing out.

Our hill, to us a giant cast
in rock, eyes at sea sail past.

But nowhere special's lee
is also where ships are mostly

and, although smudged by tides,
here is a lifetime wide.

Sometimes staring at Where again
eases the strain

of Who, looking out there's
safer. Though a lot of who is where.

What's sure is: not enough alive,
waking, I try

to keep in sight
one-off airy sleights

of place as they somehow
light up here and now.

I've inherited what I fit
almost, tried living in not on it.

Still, out there's blur
is mostly the one in here.

Look at swifts, spun
arcs bounced off reflections

of themselves in a rippled place
towards definition none trace

yet seem to aim for, stirred by flares
on water. Thirst here, now, everywhere.

In the absence of belief,
connect sun, look, with that leaf.

And there are sounds
always voicing familiar ground.

Just out of sight, human shapes
are reclaiming wired landscapes:

what's past too
prompts Where's conspiracy with Who,

and should being British strike a chord
I'll know I am abroad

where (though distance lends detachment,
little else is lent)

anyone can go, the knack
is in getting back,

Elsewhere-at-Home no nearer, the one
impossible destination.

Power Carving

(for J.M.)

With a chisel, once you'd peel back
leaves from a bird and not ransack the wood.
Then you grew ambitious: you'd speed up,
sell your work. So bought a power carving tool
("Consume timber at a touch!"), steel
cutters, a thundering dust extractor
and, hunched, vacuumed our brains.
You glanced up that last time,
shrugged. It's tricky,
advancing without losing your way or voice.

Going to work, these days I see
two youths, retarded, run past open-mouthed
who only slow to call the crossing-lady over.
Beautiful the white arm raised, the roar
smoothed out. I'd like to find
what makes them run and where, flapping
in take-off, so intent on starting
over they've disappeared into themselves.

Change

(December, 1989)

Look at the window's
tricky mirror. The same face
stares back. But from the east,
wind blows branches through —
the trees know more than you do,
framing yourself again.
Whole countries unbecome
themselves. Stripped has-beens

earn the right to green.
Make room: what's rooted
beyond self, enduring,
needs space to grow.
It would be wintry though.
You'd have to shed, remake,
hold to the chance sometime
you could break through

silence, be changed, new.
Years and a car crash back,
that fault in your head
brought quakes, rumours
the ceiling confirmed later
when tongue throbbed morse
or just plain epilepsy.
Forced rearrangement

not paid-for change.
You'd be stopped. Then
would start again, trembling
an arc of thrust like leaves.
And after reprieves
came days of giant light
effacing the pale self,
such light after blackout

as if mind had sat winter out.
Short of forced surging,
we can inch to a different season.
If they weren't stood on,
all shadows would be gone.
Better to move anyway, become
perhaps green, than stay — or
(especially) go then not come back.

Acknowledgements

Some of these poems have appeared, or are to appear,
in *Crab Creek Review, Cumberland Poetry Review,
Jacaranda Review, New England Review / Bread Loaf
Quarterly, New Mexico Humanities Review, Outposts,
Planet, Poetry Ireland, Poetry Wales, Slow Dancer,
South Dakota Review, Stand, Tar River Poetry,* and
The New Welsh Review.

Others have appeared in the anthologies *Harvest*
(Signature Books, Utah), *The Bright Field* (Carcanet)
and *The Critical Eye* (Holt, Rhinehart and Winston,
Texas).